BRIAN TURNER

PHANTOM NOISE

BLOODAXE BOOKS

ISBN: 978 1 85224 876 5

This edition first published 2010 by
Bloodaxe Books Ltd,
Highgreen,
Tarset,
Northumberland NE48 1RP.

www.bloodaxebooks.com
For further information about Bloodaxe titles
please visit our website or write to
the above address for a catalogue.

Original US edition first published 2010
by Alice James Books, Farmington, Maine
www.alicejamesbooks.org

Supported by
**ARTS COUNCIL
ENGLAND**

Cover design: Neil Astley & Pamela Robertson-Pearce.

Printed in Great Britain by
Bell & Bain Limited, Glasgow, Scotland.

CONTENTS

ACKNOWLEDGEMENTS

Phantom Noise was first published in the US in 2010 by Alice James Books. This first UK edition reprints the contents of that book, with the addition of one poem not included in the original American edition, 'On the Surgeon's Table', along with some minor amendments.

Grateful acknowledgement is made to the following journals and anthologies in which these poems appeared, sometimes in slightly different forms: *Alehouse Press*: 'Study of the Nudes by Candlelight'; *The Alhambra Poetry Calendar* (2010): 'Dar as-Salam'; *Between Water and Song: New Poets for the Twenty-First Century* (White Pine Press): 'Wading Out' and 'Guarding the Bomber'; *The Columbia Poetry Review*: 'Jundee Ameriki'; *The Cortland Review*: 'Homemade Napalm'; *The Georgia Review*: 'Wading Out'; Literary Witnesses: 'Lucky Money'; *The New York Times online*: 'Guarding the Bomber'; *The Northwest Review*: 'Stopping the American Infantry Patrol Near the Prophet Yunus Mosque in Mosul, Abu Ali Shows Them the Cloth in His Pocket', 'Mohammed Trains for the Beijing Olympics, 2008'; *The Portland Review*: '.22 Caliber'; *Southword* (Ireland): 'Eucalyptus', 'To My Unnamed Daughter', 'A Lullaby for Bullets'; *The Stinging Fly* (Ireland): 'American Internal'; Stone Canoe: 'At Lowe's Home Improvement Center'; *The Virginia Quarterly Review*: 'Unearthed by Wind', 'Perimeter Watch', 'VA Hospital Confessional', 'On the Flight to Alamosa, Colorado', 'The Discothèque', 'Ajal'.

My deepest gratitude to the following: Dan Albergotti, Donald Anderson, Doug Anderson, Siah Armajani, Stephen Barile, Aliki Barnstone, Tony Barnstone, Willis Barnstone, Sarah Barr, Paul Bellowar, Tom Bosch, Laure-Anne Bosselaar, Kevin Bowen, Kurt Brown, Kim Buchheit, Rosanne Cahn, Matt Cashion, Cyrus Cassells, Peter Catapano, Jo Chapman, Russell Conrad, Patrick Cotter, Tim Crowley, Martín Espada, Tony Fiorillo, Patsy Garoupa, Ted Genoways, Paul Guest, James Haba, Corrinne Clegg Hales, Charles Hanzlicek, James Hathaway, Lee Herrick, Garrett Hongo, Doug and Tristan Humble, T.R. Hummer, David Jackowski, Martha Jessup, Haider Al-Kabi, Marion Kelly, Maura Kennedy, Dorianne Laux, Suzie Lechtenberg, Kwang Ho

Lee, Philip Levine, Soheil Najm, Anne Marie Macari, Adrian Matejka, Khaled Mattawa, Declan Meade, Col. Tom McGuire, Sadek Mohammed, LTC John A. Nagl, Oliver de la Paz, Mike Robinson, Summer Rodman, Patricia Smith, R. Southerland, Tim Skeen, Gerald Stern, Ernesto Trejo, Charles Trimbach, Bill Tuell, Jessica Valls, Dan Veach, Bruce Weigl, Barry Wexler, Sholeh Wolpe and Steve Yarbrough.

I would like to thank the Lannan Foundation, Alison Granucci at Blue Flower Arts, the National Endowment for the Arts, the William Joiner Center for the Study of War and Social Consequences, Matt O'Donnell at From the Fishouse, Dan at Grolier Poetry Bookshop, Tim Crowley at the Marfa Bookstore, and the Kerouac Project of Orlando, Florida for their kind and generous support of my work (and for all they do to support artists).

Many thanks to Neil Astley, Julia Bouwsma, Todd Davis, Patrick Hicks, Ilya Kaminsky, Dunya Mikhail, Joe Millar, Ahmed Nussaif, April Ossmann, Carey Salerno, Lacy Simons and Ellen Doré Watson, for their guidance, insight and kind support of this work. Love and thanks to my family and friends, with special thanks to Stacey Lynn Brown, Brian Voight, and – of course – to Ilyse.

VA Hospital Confessional

Each night is different. Each night the same.
Sometimes I pull the trigger. Sometimes I don't.

When I pull the trigger, he often just stands there,
gesturing, as if saying, *Aren't you ashamed?*

When I don't, he douses himself
in gasoline, drowns himself in fire.

A dog barks in the night's illuminated green landscape
and the platoon sergeant orders me to shoot it.

Some nights I twitch and jerk in my sleep.
My lover has learned to face away.

She closes her eyes when I fuck her. I imagine
she's far away and we don't use the word *love*.

When she sleeps, helicopters
come in low over the date palms.

Men are bound on their knees, shivering
in the animal stall, long before dawn.

I whisper into their ears, saying,
Howlwin? Howlwin? Meaning, *Mortars? Mortars?*

Howl wind, motherfucker? Howl wind?
The milk cow stares with its huge brown eyes.

The milk cow wants to know
how I can do this to another human being.

I check the haystack in the corner
for a weapons cache. I check the sewage sump.

I tell no one, but sometimes late at night
I uncover rifles and bullets within me.

Other nights I drive through Baghdad.
Firebaugh. Bakersfield. Kettleman City.

Some nights I'm up in the hatch, shooting
a controlled pair into someone's radiator.

Some nights I hear a woman screaming.
Others I shoot the crashing car.

When the boy brings us a platter of fruit,
I mistake cantaloupe for a human skull.

Sometimes the gunman fires into the house.
Sometimes the gunman fires at me.

Every night it's different.
Every night the same.

Some nights I pull the trigger.
Some nights I burn him alive.

I embrace the frightful and the beautiful

AL-BAYATI

At Lowe's Home Improvement Center

Standing in aisle 16, the hammer and anchor aisle,
I bust a 50 pound box of double-headed nails
open by accident, their oily bright shanks
and diamond points like firing pins
from M-4s and M-16s.
                              In a steady stream
they pour onto the tile floor, constant as shells
falling south of Baghdad last night, where Bosch
kneeled under the chain guns of helicopters
stationed above, their tracer-fire a synaptic geometry
of light.
          At dawn, when the shelling stops,
hundreds of bandages will not be enough.

⁊➧

Bosch is walking down aisle 16 now, in full combat gear,
improbable, worn out from fatigue, a rifle
slung at his side, his left hand guiding
a ten-year-old boy who sees what war is
and will never clear it from his head.

Here, Bosch says, *Take care of him.*
I'm going back in for more.

⁊➧

Sheets of plywood drop with the airy breath
of mortars the moment they crack open
in shrapnel. Mower blades are just mower blades
and the Troy-Bilt Self-Propelled Mower doesn't resemble
a Blackhawk or an Apache. In fact, no one seems to notice
the casualty collection center Doc High is marking out
in ceiling fans, aisle 15. Wounded Iraqis with IVs
sit propped against boxes as 92 sample Paradiso fans
hover over in a slow revolution of blades.

The forklift driver over-adjusts, swinging the tines
until they slice open gallons and gallons of paint,
Sienna Dust and Lemon Sorbet and Ship's Harbor Blue
pooling in the aisle where Sgt Rampley walks through –
carrying someone's blown-off arm cradled like an infant,
handing it to me, saying, *Hold this, Turner,*
we might find who it belongs to.

ॐ

Cash registers open and slide shut
with a sound of machine guns being charged.
Dead soldiers are laid out at the registers,
on the black conveyor belts,
and people in line still reach
for their wallets. Should I stand
at the magazine rack, reading
Landscaping with Stone or *The Complete*
Home Improvement Repair Book?
What difference does it make if I choose
tumbled travertine tile, Botticino marble,
or Black Absolute granite. Outside,
palm trees line the asphalt boulevards,
restaurants cool their patrons who will enjoy
fireworks exploding over Bass Lake in July.

ॐ

Aisle number 7 is a corridor of lights.
Each dead Iraqi walks amazed
by Tiffany posts and Bavarian pole lights.
Motion-activated incandescents switch on
as they pass by, reverent sentinels of light,
Fleur De Lis and Luminaire Mural Extérieur
welcoming them to Lowe's Home Improvement Center,
aisle number 7, where I stand in mute shock,
someone's arm cradled in my own.
                              The Iraqi boy beside me
reaches down to slide his fingertip in Retro Colonial Blue,
an interior latex, before writing
T, for *Tourniquet,* on my forehead.

16

Howl Wind

I see people riding on shrieking horses,
steering clouds of sparkbelching fires
on their way to flame life out of you

MAHD AL-AADIYYA (4000 BCE)

Launched from its tube, the mortar round
accelerates to the apogee of its flight,
rising fast to what the gunners call
the high angle of hell, the round
suspended over the city lights below,
where any one of us might find ourselves
deep within the very last day of our life,
but wholly unaware of the fact – unaware
that the steel-hard visitations of death
hang from the heavens above,
and if there's someone we would kiss
goodbye, or a few words we'd rather share
than leave unspoken, then now is the time,
because just as missiles were hurled in fire
from catapults of old, a mortar round
howls a night wind over the city,
and just where it lands
we will see.

Aubade: Layover in Amsterdam

My lover turns in the California bedroom's
watery dark, arching her back from that slow

smooth glissando of heat within flesh,
our bodies rising on coiled springs

as if riding a wave of tension,
the room beneath us fading, my head leaning back,

eyes closing to the bright points of light,
my mouth filling with a long vowel

lifting into moonlight, the jet stream
blowing through my hair, the earth curving below;

rising over the cold waters of the Atlantic
to 30,000 feet, I begin to sense the imminent

descent toward the Red Lights of Amsterdam,
the clock reversing itself to the spring of 2004,

where I lie with a woman who knows
I'm a man heading back to war,

and I want her to whisper in my ear,
even in a language I've never heard before,

just to hear another human voice, just to breathe in the dark.

The Whale

It is 1970
       and the summer of love is over.

I am three years old, barefoot,
     running along the surf
near Florence, Oregon,

where an eight-ton sperm whale
    beached itself and died, the carcass
rotting now,
             an entrance carved into its massive flank
for cases of dynamite, 500 pounds of explosives
    necessary to rend open the interior
so scavengers can pick the skeleton clean –

but for me, it is the doorway to another world,
    the body of the sacred I might enter into,
its eyes drained of all but a giant benevolence,
    flukes wide as the tailfins of bombers
       overhead, my mother

hoisting me to her hip as engineers argue
    blasting caps and stand-off distance,
equations to undo the intricate puzzle
    of muscle and bone –
                  the way life waits for us all
     with great patience, the electrons orbiting
in their shells like distant planets we never see,
    the constellations which bind the universe
undone this day, at least for this one body
     beached on the sand as we witness the blast
from the sawgrass dunes,
               the sudden
   jolt of nerves as the body absorbs
the shockwave, beach-sand shot upward
    in jets of tissue and meat,
the local news reporter dropping to his knees
    to cover his head with a clipboard
   while the cameraman does the same,

my mother shielding me with her torso
    turned away from the blast

  and I remember everyone smiling
afterward, laughing, each of us amazed
    the day a god was blown to pieces on the beach
      and we all walked away from it, unscathed.

Chinese Ink Brush Painting

There are days when the mallards
slip under the oily surface

the way the eye's glossy circle
welcomes light, the weapon's reticle

burned onto your retinas
in a false negative

so that now you view everything
with hash marks denoting elevation,

lines superimposed over the nipple's
aureole, the scapula with its play

of bone-articulated shadow.
It is how heavyweight paper

absorbs the fluid, the animal
shape, if not the animal itself.

❧

Slender beaks stretch the skin
as you sleep. You open one eye, twist

the brush to disturb the trance, catch birds
shaking the cold from their feathers –

these larger birds of the shoreline,
bony knees above the water's

surface, koi brushing shins
with curious whiskers, cat-like

insouciance, though the herons' eyes
dart furtive into the cage-work of reeds,

where insurgents row a fishing boat
as though they are fishermen, weapons

out of view, alluded to in the rifling
brushwork of reeds fallen on water, burnt umber.

≈▲

This next piece: the vision of a crow held down
on a steel table, lab coats and Plexiglas visors,

doctors with precision tools, the beak
pried open in place. The bird's eyes

scan the room, just as you would
were you strapped to an operating table

in a fluorescent cell, bright instruments
clamping the thick of your tongue

to hold it in place, the heat of the scalpel
splicing the fleshy tip into two, a searing

nerve-hit volt, a recognition in the centers of the brain
where language composes the syntax

of pain, the lung's breath given a transformative speech,
what the doctors call *a necessary intelligence*.

Sleeping in Dick Cheney's Bed

Rampart Lodge, USAF Academy, 2009

It's unnerving how comfortable this is:
NORAD watching over the bedroom, Colorado
mule deer chewing the dawn outside as I dream
I'm wading thigh-high into the North Platte River,
wearing rubber waders, casting a handmade fly
with a whip-like, graceful sling of the line
until I fall back, plunge into the cold rushing
white water, my eyes blurred hard
under the sun's interrogations – Cheney's hands
like a preacher's delivering me deeper into the truth,
with a gasp of air, a flash of light, to be plunged back down
the way he offers midges and bloodworms and rusty scuds
to the cloudy river, running 1400 cubic feet per second,
until I cough up the fictional and beg for the heartland's
fluid clarity, salvation, the charity of forgiveness, *anything*
to unravel the dream and return me back my California bed,
my lover beside me and not this stale man's breath
clinging to the Egyptian cotton sheets, the hanging curtains,
the flaring light of Colorado Springs where Cheney slept
in this very bed, both of us held by the same coiling
box spring, goose down pillows cupping our heads
gently into sleep, the reddening glow of Mars
rising over the horizon, dead skin sloughed off
to coat my own skin at an invisible level, and still –
what does it say about me, that the Pinot Grigio
tasted so good on my tongue, and that
I struggled to be a sergeant tonight,
speaking to the officer corps in a theater
filled with 1600 listening faces – as I spoke
about rape, death, and murder – what does it say about me
that I can return to Cheney's room after midnight,
strip my clothes off to curl in the bed
where he too has slept, the sheets a sublime reprieve
for my tired frame, the night a perfection of sleep.

Viking 1

Viking Lander 1 made its final transmission to Earth
NOVEMBER 11, 1982

On approach to Mars, dune fields in the distance,
the spacecraft descends within a storm of dust
before landing on the Golden Plain, Chryse Planitia,
which is a vast and stony desert, a graveyard
of shadows cast sanguine in their repose.

Cameras click in shuttered housings. The landscape
a pornographic scene caught in apertures
opened wide: sand tables in their martial aspect,
compass points, barchan dunes, the far horizon's body line
in rocky silhouette, where Earth is a small, warm light
rising zenith blue beyond the dusk, where I am still a boy,
barefoot on the wet grass of the San Joaquin valley,
the millions of miles between made closer by opposition.

In the old days, they say the desert Arabs hung lanterns
high in the date palms, a guide for friends and strangers
traveling by night. And maybe that's what I'm doing
as I search for lamps in the night's vast amphitheater,
even if I don't know how to put it into words –
I'm searching for the face on Mars, so much like our own,
made from dust and to dust returning, the wind's erosion
calling into the void with that brutal instrument, pain.
And like so many before me, I listen.
I want to hear how the great questions posed by ruin
are given the elegant response of stone.

How we, like Aphrodite, are seduced.

Perimeter Watch

I lock the doors tonight, check the bolts twice
just to make sure. Turn off all the lights.
Only the fan blades rotate above, slow as helicopters
winding down their oily gears.
                            Water buffalo
chew the front lawn, snorting. When the sprinklers
switch on, white cowbirds lift up from the grass
with heavy wing-beats, a column of feathers
rising over my rooftop, their wing-tips
backlit by the moon.
                      Through venetian blinds
I see the Iraqi prisoners in that dank cell at Firebase Eagle
staring back at me. They say nothing, just as they did
in the winter of 2004, shivering in the piss-cold dark,
on scraps of cardboard, staring.
                          Snipers traverse the skyline
from the neighbor's rooftop. Helicopters on station,
fifteen minutes out. And it's difficult to tell the living
from the dead, walking the dim elephant grass, papyrus thickets
lining the asphalt streets. I see Bosch, my old rifleman,
sleepwalking – on fire and unaware of it.
                           I see the Stryker,
Ghost 3, parked at the curb. I know the guys inside
watch Iraqi women in the white-hot lens
of the gun-mount camera, eager for the smolder
of their sex. A minivan idles with passengers dying inside
while down the street, an explosion sets off
the neighbor's car alarm.
                    Then, quiet.
The wounded wait with great patience for Doc High,
who treats them by the pool in the backyard,
where I can see the Turkish cook with shrapnel
in the back of his head, his mouth still foaming.
Beside him, the dead infant from that cold blue morning
in the orange groves of Balad, while in the pool
a battalion scout floats face down
in the current.
                  Where is my M-4? My smoke grenades?
My flak vest and plates of body armor? I wander the house

searching for them, hear the 12-year-old voice just outside
the front door – *Where is my father? Let free my father.*
My father no bad man. Let go my father.

When I dial 911,
the operator tells me to use proper radio procedure,
reminding me that my call sign is *Ghost 1-3 Alpha*,
and that it's time, long past time, to unlock the door
and let these people in.

Illumination Rounds

Will the girl find a bed among the stones?
Will the fighter find a trench?
SAADI YOUSSEF

Parachute Flares drift in the burn time
of dream, their canopies deployed
in the sky above our bed. My lover

sleeps as Iraqi translators shuffle
in through the doorway – visiting
as loved ones might visit a hospital room,
ill at ease, each of them holding
their sawn-off heads in hand.

Wordless, they wait for me
to dress in my desert fatigues,
my aid pouch with painkillers

of little help in sewing the larynx back,
though I try anyway, suture by suture.

&

She finds me at 3 A.M., shoveling
the grassy turf in our backyard, digging
three feet by six, determined to dig deep.
We need to help them, if only with a coffin,
I say, and if she could love me enough
to trust me, to not cover her mouth
in shock or recognition, her hair lit up
in moonlight; if she could shovel
beside me, straining with the weight
each blade lifts in its gunmetal sheen,
then she'd begin to see them – the war dead –
how they stand under lime trees and ash,
papyrus and stone in their hands.

She stares at these blurry figures
in silhouette, the very young and very old
among them, and with a gentle hand

29

stays the shovel I hold, to say –
We should invite them into our home.
We should learn their names, their history.
We should know these people
we bury in the earth.

ɞ

I'm out on patrol again, driving
Blackstone to Divisidero, Route Tampa
to Bridge Number Four, California
to the neighborhoods of Mosul, each stoplight
an increment, a block away from home
and a block closer to the August night
replaying in my head.

I wish I could tell you
I've come to save someone,
I've come with bandages and IVs
for the wounded –
                    but it's all bullshit:
I'm here for the turning, that rooftop
swiveling of lasers and tracer-fire,
gunshots echoing years later, the incoherent
screaming I've translated a thousand times over,
driving until I finally understand
who it is I'm supposed to kill.

Puget Sound

Clouds shield the stars where jellyfish
drift in the harbor, and facing the water,
in an idling Chrysler, windshield
glazed by rain, Private Reynolds,

who in six weeks will deploy to Iraq
for the first time, white-knuckles
the cord, the ends wrapped tight
around each hand. His wife stops breathing –
her larynx exhausted within a tunnel of light.

Daybreak. Workday. Night.
For four days she drifts in the Sound.
Barges ferry lumber to the pulp mill
and dockside fishermen cast lines
for rock cod and eel. Joggers,
mothers pushing strollers, teens
on rollerblades listening to music
through headphones – all pass by.
A golden retriever named Pepper
discovers her – a woman with eyes
mirroring the sea, washed and transformed,
grayed-out by what she's seen.

Al-A'imma Bridge

This will leave a scar in our souls...
PRESIDENT JALAL TALABANI

They fall from the bridge into the Tigris –
    they fall from railings or tumble down, shoved by panic,
        by those in the crushing weight behind them,
    mothers with children, seventy-year-old men
        clawing at the blue and empty sky, which is too beautiful;

    some focus on the bridgework as they fall, grasp
        the invisible rope which slips through their fingers,
    some palm-heel the air beneath them, pressing down
        as their children swim in the oxygen beside them,
    lives blurring with no time to make sense, some
        so close to shore they smash against the rocks;

    the pregnant woman who twists
        in a corkscrew of air, flipping upside down,
    the world upended, her black dress
        a funeral banner rippling in the wind,
    her child never given a name;

they fall beside Shatha and Cantara and Sabeen,
    Hakim, Askari, and Gabir – unraveling years
        and memory, struggling to keep heads above water,
    the hard shock sweeping them downstream
        as Askari fights to gain the shoreline
    where emerald flags furl in sunlight,
        and onlookers wave frantic arms
    at Gabir, who holds the body of a dead child
        he doesn't know, and it is only 11:30 A.M.,
And this is how we die, he thinks
    on a day as beautiful as this;

and Shatha, who feels the river's cold hands
    pulling her under, remembers once loving
the orange flowers opening on the hillsides
    of Mosul, how she lay under slow clouds
drifting in history's bright catalogue;

they fall with 500 pound bombs and mortars,
    laser-guided munitions directing the German Luftwaffe
        from 1941, Iraqi jets and soldiers from the Six-Day War,
        the Battle of Karbala, the one million who died fighting Iran;

and Alexander the Great falls, and King Faisal,
        and the Israeli F-16s that bombed the reactor in '81,
        and the Stele of the Vultures comes crumbling,
            the Tower of Samarra, the walled ruins of Nineveh;

the Babylonians and Sumerians and Assyrians join them,
    falling from the bridge with Ibn Khaldun's torn pages,
    The Muqaddimah – that classic Islamic history of the world,
    and Sheherazade falls too, worn out, exhausted
        from her life-saving work, made speechless by the scale of war,
    and Ali Baba with an AK-47 beside her;

    whiskey and vodka, pirated Eastern European porn videos
        the kids hawk to soldiers – the *freaky freaky* they call it,
    and foil-wrapped packages of *heroin, heroin*
        thrown to the river;

The year 1956 slides under, along with '49 and '31 and '17.
    the month of October, the months of June, July, and August,
        the many months to follow, each day's exquisite light,
    the snowfall in Mosul, the photographs a family took
        of children rolling snowballs, throwing them
    before licking the pink cold from their fingertips;

Years unravel like filaments of straw, bleached gold
    and given to the water, 1967 and 1972, 2001 and 2002:
    What will we remember? What will we say of these?

it awakens the dead from the year 1258
    who cannot believe what is happening here, *Not a shot fired* –
        our internalised panic deeply set by years of warfare,
    the siege and adrenaline always at the surface, prepared;

the dead from the year 1258 read from ancient scrolls
    cast into the river from the House of Wisdom,
    the eulogies of nations given water's swift erasure;

and the dead watch as they are swept downstream –
    witness to the soft, tender lips of the river fish
        who kiss the calves and fingertips of these newly dead,
    curious to see how lifeless bodies stare hard
        into the dark envelopment, hands
    waving to the far shore;

the *djinn* awaken from their slumber
    to watch the dead pass by, one fixed
        with an odd smile, the drawn-out vowel
    of a word left unfinished, and they want to hold these dead
        close and tight, the lung's last reserve given
    as a whisper of bubbles for the ear held up to it;
the *djinn* swim to reach the bony ankles of Sabeen,
        the muscled Askari, clasping to stop them
    from this tragic undertaking;

and some are nearly saved by others diving in
    to rescue the terrified and the stunned,
        but drown beneath a woman's soaked abaya;

and the Tigris is filling with the dead, filling
    with bricks from Abu Ghraib, burning vehicles
        pushed from Highway 1 with rebar, stone, metal,
    with rubble from the Mosque bombed in Samarra,
        guard towers and razor wire imprisoning Tikrit,
    it fills with the pipelines of money;

    marketplace bombs, roadside bombs, vehicle-driven
        bombs, and the bombs people make of themselves;

Gilgamesh can do nothing, knows that each life is the world
    dying anew, each body the deep pull of currents below, lost,
        and lost within each – the subtle, the sublime, the horrific,
    the mundane, the tragic, the humorous and the erotic – lost,

    unstudied in text books, courses on mathematics,
        the equations quantifying fear,
    or the stoppage of time this eternal moment creates,
        unwritten history, forgotten in American hallways, but still –

give them flowers from the hills, flowers from the Shanidar cave,
    where mourning has a long history, where someone in the last Ice Age
        gathered a bouquet – give daisies and hyacinths
    to this impossible moment, flowers to stand for the lips
        unable to kiss them, each in their own bright beauty, flowers
    that may light the darkness, as they march deeper into the earth.

Helping Her Breathe

Subtract each sound. Subtract it all.
Lower the contrailed decibels of fighter jets
below the threshold of human hearing.
Lower the skylining helicopters down
to the subconscious and let them hover
like spiders over a film of water.

Silence the rifle reports. The hissing
bullets wandering like strays
through the old neighborhoods.
Let the dogs rest their muzzles
as the voices on telephone lines
pause to listen, as bats hanging
from their roosts pause to listen,
as all of Baghdad listens.

Dip the rag in the pail of water
and let it soak full. It cools exhaustion
when pressed lightly to her forehead.
In the slow beads of water sliding
down the skin of her temples –
the hush we have been waiting for.

She is giving birth in the middle of war –
the soft dome of a skull begins to crown
into our candlelit mystery. And when
the infant rises through quickening muscle
in a guided shudder, slick in the gore
of birth, vast distances are joined,
the brain's landscape equal to the stars.

Guarding the Bomber

His legs gone, bandaged at midfemur,
he palms the invisible above him like a conductor
in difficult passages of fluorescent streaming light,
two gauze-wrapped stumps directing movement
from his shoulders as I wipe salt from his lips
with a wet rag, check the feeding tube, the IV
in his neck, listen to his morphined Arabic
as I imagine him lying in debris
and settling dust, his brain snapping back
into momentary consciousness, realising
that his feet – fastened in their sandals –
wait for him across the room, and that his hands –
driven beyond the body – still negotiate
black wires and hot wires, arming
explosives in a 155mm shell casing,
his body unable to sweat as he works
beyond me and my thoughts of his Paradise,
wondering if the virgins will care for him
as I do, changing his bedpan, bathing him
with sponges and reassurances in English –
a language he hates, its vowels
a sheen of oil on steel – no,
he's far beyond my rifle and desert fatigues,
his dexterous ghost limbs tending the fire,
and whether I want to admit it or not
the explosives continue around him, his arms
elbow-deep in the blue flame and heat,
reaching in to save me.

Phantom Noise

There is this ringing hum   this
bullet-borne language   ringing
shell-fall and static   this late-night
ringing of threadwork and carpet   ringing
hiss and steam   this wing-beat
of rotors and tanks   broken
bodies ringing in steel   humming these
voices of dust   these years ringing
rifles in Babylon   rifles in Sumer
ringing these children their gravestones
and candy   their limbs gone missing   their
static-borne television   their ringing
this eardrum   this rifled symphonic   this
ringing of midnight in gunpowder and oil   this
brake pad gone useless   this muzzle-flash singing   this
threading of bullets in muscle and bone   this ringing
hum   this ringing hum   this
ringing

Zippo

Just to prove his point, Stoltman
unscrews the tanker's fuel cap, grinning
the way he always does, a cigarette
dangling from his lips, a feigned concentration
on his forehead – though under tissue and bone
a focus deeper than the prank at work,
calculating flash points and fire points, diesel
and flame, the necessary heat to ignite
his life, the paperwork with his wife's signature
sealed by the hard-pressed pen –
Stoltman flips open the hinged metal,
its polished chrome worn by sweat and grime,
his free hand dunked to the wrist in fuel, soaked
and dripping he pulls it out in the morning chill,
and when he strikes the thumbwheel to flint the wick's naphtha,
nobody moves, nobody stops him, nobody says a word,
because we all want to see if Stoltman will burn.

Homemade Napalm
Winter, 1978

We followed a recipe from *The Poor Man's*
James Bond – my father mixing gasoline
with bone meal and Ivory soap, teaching me
to shave a bar of soap with the flattened edge
of the blade, my hands stung pink
in the morning cold.
                  He drank coffee,
saying nothing of my grandfather,
the Marine, Guadalcanal, the flamethrower
carried on his back. He didn't need to.
There was a thick fog that morning
he pulled the igniter and the gel
burst into a flame, sucking oxygen
from the air, a strange kind of fire
turning inward on itself.
                My grandfather
took shots of Kentucky bourbon. My father
downed a twelve-pack each night.
And it was hard to understand why
I'd find him in the living room sometimes,
late, long after I'd gone to bed, waking
to the sound of Josh White singing the blues
in the old-time vinyl, but I began to learn –
to be a man is to carry things inside
no one would ever understand,
things better left unsaid; sung about,
maybe, those rare nights in winter, alone,
the world fuming with alcohol,
spinning in the blue dark.

Bruce Lee's *Enter the Dragon*

I drank a Seagram's Seven and Seven on 7/7/77,
when I was only ten and my Mom a bartender
at the Airport Marina lounge – where I mostly drank
Grasshoppers and Roy Rogers while Ed Burke
sang 'Mr Bojangles' and danced a slow shuffle
like he always did after Happy Hour,
six to ten P.M., Sunday through Thursday.

I liked the pale-green Grasshoppers best,
mainly because I liked watching *Kung Fu*
with David Carradine as Kwai Chang Caine,
Master Po demonstrating wisdom –
Close your eyes – what do you hear?
I hear the water. I hear the birds.
Do you hear your own heartbeat?
Do you hear the grasshopper at your feet?

When she could afford a sitter, I'd stay
at the Alexander's – a family who ate chicken and rice
even more often than we ate ham hocks and beans.
The oldest son was rarely around, but he wore
enormous aviator shades, looked like Bruce Lee
driving up in his T-top Camaro, canary yellow,
like sunlight. When he'd leave again
I'd try to beat up little Ralphie, the youngest,
by utilising the black belt knowledge of karate
I assumed I'd learned by visual osmosis, *film study style*,
my own version of the Jeet Kune Do combat form.

One night, after the 'Star Spangled Banner' played
and the multicolored bars lit up the television,
the room filled with a comforting low crackle of static,
Mrs Alexander startled Dana and me, catching us
sleeping side by side – Dana
(who once taught me how to French kiss)
using my arm like a pillow, her face
resting on my shoulder, one leg

draped over mine, curled into me,
both of us lying the way I'd seen couples
do it in the movies, blue smoke the only thing missing,
a Marlboro in my lips, burnt down to the filter.

Lucky Money

It is 1971.
                At Willie Lum's Hong Kong Restaurant
I am four years old and this is my very first job:
   carry the steaming tea by the bamboo handle,
deliver it to Willie Lum's ancient mother.
   It is much more difficult than a simple balancing
of heat over distance. There's the back kitchen, gleaming
   in chrome, knives, the crackling of fluorescent lights.
There's the old man at the sink strangling the dishes,
   the dead look he has for children, that bang
of pots in the slosh of the tub, and the back door,
   how to squeeze past its riveted metal sheets
to the most difficult of all,
                       the bridge, the plank –
that weathered twelve-foot board which spans
   the ledge of the restaurant's back door
to the porch of his mother's trailer and below that,
   seven feet down, chained on a leash of stainless steel –
the bullmastiff, gnashing its teeth, its larynx
   growling from the deep pit of midnight,
the nerves of my skin aware of the bats
   skimming the oak trees, walnuts
forming in cerebral shells – and I walked out
   into the universe, the frightening unknown beauty of it,
my hair turned electric. This is where I learned to walk the line
   over bristling fur, the rough lungs of a language
calling up from the depths below, all I must ignore
   if I want to cross over, a boy of four with a pot of tea
for an old woman buried in afghans, lit by Chinese lanterns,
an ancient one who gives me red and gold envelopes,
   who says *Lucky money. No spendee. Lucky money.*

On the Flight to Alamosa, Colorado

At 10,000 feet, the lights of Denver
fade, pilots check their gauges.
The Beechcraft's engines thrum my ears
as elevation and cabin pressure block out
passengers in conversation behind me,
my view a distorted globe,
my reflection in it moonless, culpable.

Once again, I'm in the belly of a C-130
with Fiorillo's and Hathaway's and Jax's
silence, cold rifles in our hands,
the Highway of Death guiding us
to the airstrip at Anaconda, 210
bullets sleeping on my chest.

We haunt the streets of Balad
at midnight, kicking in doors
and raiding houses, separating the men
from women and children, flex-cuffing
wrists and sandbagging their heads,
searching block by block, house to house,
in sewage sumps, animal stalls, sacks of flour,
searching for all we have left behind –
the missing arms, the missing legs, the dead nerves
in Bosch's hand, the blood drained from Miller's head.

Wading Out

Ad Duluiyah, Iraq

We're crossing an open field, sweating in December's heat,
with 1st Squad covering from the brush to our left.
I could be shot dead by a sniper, easily –
this could be the ground where I bleed out in 90 seconds,
but it won't be. There's a patch of still water
I'm about to walk into as I always do,
too much adrenaline and momentum in my stride,
boots sinking ankle-deep and still I slog forward,
M-4 held up over my head. Fiorillo sinks to his knees
to my right – then backs up, makes it out
of the septic runoff I'm up to my thighs in,
the stench filling my nostrils, and it's funny enough
once the mission's done, *Turner running in to swim*,
but no one's laughing anymore, the months turning
into years gone by and still I'm down there slogging
shoulder-deep into the shit, my old platoon
with another year of bullets and mortars and missions
dragging them further in, my lieutenant so far down
I can't reach him anymore, my squad leader hunting
for souls that would mark him and drag him under
completely, better than any bottle of whiskey.
And I keep telling myself that if I walk far enough
or long enough someday I'll come out the other side.
But will Jax and Bosch and my lieutenant make it, too?
If one day we find ourselves poolside in California,
the day as bright as this one, how will we hose ourselves off
to remove the stench, standing around a barbeque
talking football – how?

(after Bruce Weigl)

White Phosphorus

When Larry Jr nails a catfish
to the trunk of a black tupelo,

the summer tanagers and dark-eyed juncos
pause in their singing to the afternoon,

and it isn't the hammer or the nail
driving it in, it's that low vowel of pain

stretching out over the Arkansas River
and into the sway of pines, a sound that travels

along Dollarway Road and on into town,
where Ray and Suzanne have forgotten

how to talk with one another, steam
curling over their coffee at the diner.

Across the street, the old man Jackson
loses his train of thought, straining

to recall the year 1928, the shade tree
where Uncle Harold was buried

after the gas of the Argonne Forest
finally took him down. It's like this

at International Paper, and at the County Courthouse.
It's like this in the back parking lot of the Duck Inn's

Chateau Lounge, where Marlene has finally
broken down, her forehead on the steering wheel.

Even in the soybean fields and poultry farms
outside of town. This pause, this quiet recognition.

Here. In Pine Bluff, Arkansas, where it's made.

.22 Caliber

It's a Saturday. My father out in the garage
with a ball peen hammer, tamping.
Assembling a zip gun, teaching me
to clamp the small diameter pipe
to form a smooth-bore barrel,
bracket and finishing nail
as hammer and firing pin.

1981. The Soviets fight in Afghanistan.
Magazine racks carry *Guns & Ammo*,
*Penthouse, Hustler, Shooting Times
& Country Magazine*. It is a world
filled with ballistics, armor, lethal flights
of small metal rounds, spinning.
On the back cover of *Soldier of Fortune*
an armed mujahedeen lying in the prone
on a rocky overlook, the coupon below him
promising: *Buy a Bullet, Kill a Commie*.

Reload: I pull the hammer back
to fire over and over at paper targets
with their circles driven inward,
an exercise in muscle memory.
I am learning how to connect
with the small dark silence
carried within the center of all things.

Green Alexandrine

At Divisidero and Olive, the squad cars
haven't arrived, they're still blocks away with sirens
switched on, the radio traffic announcing codes
of trauma – *one vehicle, injuries unknown* –
while I stand here, amazed, at the intersection
of pain, the traffic backed up in all directions,
a thin haze of exhaust drifting over the scene
where a Plymouth revs its engine, the wheel hub stripped
on the driver's side, scorching the asphalt as sparks
pinwheel out as if from the hooves of a maddened
bull, the car's metal hood ruckled from the grillwork
smashed into the stoplight's pole, over and over,
revving the engine, the light somehow stuck on red,
juicing the accelerator with the brake pad
clamped down, as pawn shops, money lenders, liquor stores
stand witness behind wrought iron bars, the man now
in a searing kind of rage that takes a lifetime
to hone into an art form like this, a public
spectacle, clear as my great-grandfather, Carter,
beating a heifer to death with the twisted branch
from an oak tree, that kind of clarity of rage,
which moves a young woman to step out from her car,
to walk carefully into the headlights and noise,
her voice – the smallest drops of honey I tasted
as a boy – her soft words saying *Are you alright?*

On the Surgeon's Table

Colonel Gustafson, you've done all you could.
Let the nurses disconnect clamps, retractors,
suction tubes. Let them sterilise the scalpels
as you try to forget the degloving of the scalp,
the guillotine amputation at the thigh.

You've done all you could for this one,
Colonel. Go to your bunk. Sleep awhile.
Try not to dream the charnel visitations
of the dead, the many questions they have,
as one holds the clear plastic covering
over his irrigated abdomen, another
staring into the blind and newfound
darkness within the skull, while the amputee
asks how he could die of shock
when the bleeding was controlled, volume
resuscitation begun, and *What, Doctor –*
what have you done with my leg?

Unearthed by Wind

When the winds drive south from Anatolia,
down through western Iraq and into the Kuwaiti
borderlands, the dunes shift in waves, an ocean
cresting in a swirl of dust the camels traverse
at nightfall. The wind presses on, curving
over parietal bones, smoothing them
like river stones where no water runs –
grain by grain an entire skull
emerging, its hourglass sockets
staring out at the world once more.

By companies, by battalions, these skeletons
rise slowly from the earth, dressed
in moonlight and shadow, limbs
pointing to the ancient constellations,
the far horizon, cold mountains
to the north. They chart their way
by the fires of nomads, imagining
wives and children grown old
these long years apart, how they will rest
once they return, wordless.

Some years they spend buried in sand.
In others they ask no quarter of the wind,
a counsel of ravens on their collarbones. They follow
trails of jet exhaust, which line the heavens.
They walk toward cities of light.

Madinat Al-Salam

Mother of the world, mistress of nations, heaven on earth,
city of peace, dome of Islam

YAKUT AL-HAMAWI

Ash blackened the sky in 1258, blood
ran in the rivers of Dajla and Farat,
the House of Wisdom burned to the ground
and the caliph was trampled to death by horses.

This was ancient Baghdad, July, and hot.
After 50 days of siege and 40 days of plunder
800,000 lay dead in the streets, beheaded
by Mongols, many bodies thrown to the river.

Some hid in wells and sewers.
Later, they rose from the stench
to walk the wailing streets, where wild dogs
slept with tongues panting, bellies swollen.

Downriver, villagers stood at the banks
where bodies drifted past, learning
from water's deep and rapid transport
how the dead come in constant supply.

And if we could stand among them,
as bodies blacken in flame, plume upward,
smoke flattening against heaven – if we could stand
in the House of Wisdom as the invaders

darken the river with texts and scrolls,
the old stories burning around us,
the very frame itself catching fire –
what would we have to say of loss?

Maybe we'd begin to question the word
beauty, no matter what form it is recorded in –
cuneiform, papyrus, stone.

Stopping the American Infantry Patrol Near
the Prophet Yunus Mosque in Mosul, Abu Ali Shows
Them the Cloth in His Pocket

Do you see this weathered strip of cloth, the golden threads
of its embroidery – how inconsequential it must appear to you,
only a strip of cloth – but my friends, this silk and cotton dyed black
once draped over the Black Stone; it is from the *Kiswah*,
and it is only with me now because my father made the long journey
to the *Kaaba*, to The House of God, and walked the circles
as the angels once circled God's throne; he kissed
that Black Stone, and ran between the hills, as one must,
before you were even born; his pilgrimage
part of our religion, something I have not yet done,
this war of no help in that, believe me.

When you address me, do not call me *Hajji*,
I have not been so fortunate – and you?
You do not understand the words you speak.

Tell Me, Beautiful One, from Where Did the Lord Bring You?

The minibus engines idle with the low drone
of bees working in boxes of honey.
The driver, Salim, slumps over the wheel
with bullets lodged in his head and chest,
the radio with its fretless lute, its hour glass
drum made of wood, sends music
out over the shoulder of the road
and into the lemon trees beyond.

Ra'ed – what are you thinking
as these fifty men kneel on the hardpan
close to the Iranian border, each of them
lying face down when ordered.
Resting the muzzle over the upper torso,
leveling the barrel as sweat beads
on the backs of their necks,
the late afternoon sun in a suspended fall
over the horizon at dusk, bright
as any childhood memory they might recall
from the mind's bittersweet storehouse –

how can you pull the trigger
seeing how they flinch at the bullet's report,
how they rock and pray in the dirt
as you work your way down the row,
shooting men you may have smiled or waved at
when you were just a boy sitting in the bed
of your grandfather's truck, men who climbed
date palms and sang old love songs,
saying *Ma tkuli ya hilu min wen Allah jibec*
as they cut each sweet and sticky bunch of fruit.

Insignia

One in three female soldiers will experience
sexual assault while serving in the military.

She hides under a deuce n' half this time – sleeping
on a roll of foam, draped in mosquito netting. Sandflies

hover throughout the night. She sleeps under vehicle exhaust
and heat, dreaming of mortars buried beside her, three stripes

painted on each cold tube, a rocker of yellow hung below.
It's you she's dreaming of, Sergeant – she'll dream of you

for years to come. If she makes it out of this country alive,
which she probably will. You will be the fire and the hovering

breath. Not the sniper. Not the bomber in the streets. You.
So I'm here to ask this one night's reprieve.

Let her sleep tonight. Let her sleep. Pause a moment
under the gibbous moon. Smoke. The gin your wife sent

from New Jersey, colored mint green with food dye
disguised in a bottle of mouthwash: take a long swig of it.

Take the edge out of your knuckles. Let it blur your vision
into a tremor of lights. The explosions in the distance

are not your own. In these long hours before dawn,
on the banks of the Tigris river, let her sleep.

In her dream, your eyes are pools of rifle oil.
You unsheathe the bayonet from its scabbard

while she waits. On a mattress of sand and foam, there
in the motor pool, she waits to kiss bullets into your mouth.

Mohammed Trains for the Beijing Olympics, 2008

In the 69 kilogram weight class,
the Bulgarian, Boevski, is the world
record-holder. He cannot be beaten.
At least, not by Sawara Mohammed.
Mohammed, at 26, has shoveled cement
longer than he cares to remember. In Arbil,
in Kurdish northern Iraq, he strains hard
to lift the barbell with its heavy plates,
round as the wheels of chariots – then, muscles give
and the wheels bounce in dust before him. No,
he cannot defeat the Bulgarian.

The problem is in lifting weight over distance.
It isn't a matter of iron, or of will.
In Beijing, Boevski's records will go
unnoticed, because Mohammed is training now
to lift the city of Arbil, with its people;
his quadriceps and posterior chain
straining, the muscles tremoring to lift
the Euphrates and Tigris both, mountains
of the north, deserts of the west, Basra,
Karbala, Ramadi, Tikrit, Mosul,
three decades of war and the constant suffering
of millions – this is what Sawara lifts,
and no matter what effort he makes, he will fail
completely, and the people will love him for it.

A Lullaby for Bullets

Tomorrow is made of shrapnel
and blood. There will come a time
when the trigger calls you out quickly
to the streets. And as you leave the barrel,
I can't promise you won't kill the man
who has waited all his life for the answer
to this moment, but if you lean to the right,
if you lean back and look as hard as you can
for that mountain you came from, sunlight
warming the pines, clouds approaching
from the north with a gift of silence,
if you do this you might just graze
the man's temple, so close you might hear
his name, the humming of blood
over bone, the many voices
within, the years to come.

The Discothèque

(for Tony Lagouranis)

Loaded down with prisoners after another night's raid
we pulled into the Mosul airbase, the men gagged,
zip-tied, blindfolded with engineer tape.

Forsman ate a Snickers up in the hatch
while everybody else slept shoulder to shoulder,
1st Platoon's radio silent of chatter, humming in static.

I held a 9 mm pistol in my hand, watched
how the prisoners' heads slumped in resignation,
one of them mumbling a slow rocking of prayer.

And I didn't feel a thing. I just wanted to sleep,
to wake and find myself in California –
anywhere else but here.

We turned them over to the MPs, who looked bored
of caffeine and paperwork as I filled out the depositions,
the Iraqis shunted into holding pens of wire.

I remember complaining once about The Discothèque,
that nearby container I mistook for an on-base club –
Where the pogues chill out, I said, *those fucking pogues*.

From that metal box shrouded in a camouflage netting
I never heard the screaming. I never heard the breaking of men.
I heard only music – guitars from distorted speakers.

ࣸ

The deposition forms didn't have a space
for women, who sat huddled together
in the darkness of the front room, sobbing.

Through night vision goggles they appeared
glaucous green, luminous and unnatural.
One of them – with cat's eyes of light – saw me.

The men of military age were bound, silenced
in another room. I numbered them with a Sharpie
penned on the white tape of their blindfolds.

Of the many depositions I wrote,
the many sentences I framed in careful precision,
how many were translated into Arabic?

Farid, Hasan, Mohammed, Abdullah, Jafar.
How many have heard my words spoken in court?
The Accuser. The Professor. Sgt Turner.

Late at night, Jackowski and I taped the flex charge
to the house gate. I unspooled the shock tube, removed
the safety. Hathaway radioed the countdown – and at *zero* –

I pulled the pin. It was me, Sgt Turner,
who cracked the night open with explosives
and wrote it all down, word by word.

                              ❧

It's been four years. In Poland, on the Baltic coast,
I rent a flat from Darick and Goshe. Fish and black coffee
for breakfast. Read Seife's *Zero: The Biography*

of a Dangerous Idea. And when I climb to the peak
of the coastal dunes in the Slowinski National Park,
I find nothing but wind, sand, the blue sea driven inward.

Jundee Ameriki

At the VA hospital in Long Beach, California,
Dr Sushruta scores open a thin layer of skin
to reveal an object traveling up through muscle.
It is a kind of weeping the body does, expelling
foreign material, sometimes years after injury.
Dr Sushruta lifts slivers of shrapnel, bits
of coarse gravel, road debris, diamond
points of glass – the minutiae of the story
reconstructing a cold afternoon in Baghdad,
November of 2005. The body offers aged cloth
from an *abaya* dyed in blood, shards of bone.
And if he were to listen intently, he might hear
the roughened larynx of this woman calling up
through the long corridors of flesh, saying
Allah al Akbar, before releasing
her body's weapon, her dark and lasting gift
for this *jundee Ameriki*, who carries fragments
of the war inscribed in scar tissue,
a deep, intractable pain, the dull grief of it
the body must learn to absorb.

American Internal

Down in the hole, down in the clay and mud,
we dig. The noon sun hot on our backs
as we bend to the task, as if digging
down into our own shadows
with the stained shovels of our hands,
digging until someone gasps – *another*,
they have discovered *another*; with pale eyes,
the dead faces rooted with worms and stone,
brassy shells of bullets in their mouths,
hands reaching for what no one can see above,
as if desperate to embrace us. We raise each
carefully from the earth, the bodies of men
dressed in sandals and *thawbs*,
wet robes of cotton dyed by clay,
and women, like the one I lift now,
how her hair unravels in a sheen
of copper, cold as water in my palms.

To My Unnamed Daughter

You would've turned twelve this year,
some time late November. When the rains come.

When the Tule fog starts to lift off the San Joaquin river,
drifting out over the orange groves with their fruit

frozen solid on the hard-packed ground, old tires
at the ends of rows lit with gasoline fires

to keep them warm. When I was twelve
my brother and I climbed our shingled rooftop,

looked out over country houses in a sea of fog,
with only their chimneys visible in the distance

as they, like strange flagless ships, fire smoke trailing,
steamed toward the far horizon. Everything

seemed possible. History was still being made.
We talked of riding Chinese junks in the Yellow Sea,

Arab *dhows* in the Indian Ocean, off the coast of Africa,
entire continents just waiting for us to explore.

I never told my brother about you. He's had enough –
his fourth child turned blue with a strangling cord

at birth, the nineteen months spent waiting for him
to die, and people saying *Such a beautiful child, that Ethan.*

And yet, my unborn, you never even had a name.
Just a month when you would've been born, and me, waiting.

Ajal

– the appointed time of death which Muslims believe God has determined for every individual; it cannot be delayed or hastened.

There are ninety-nine special names for God,
my son, and not so long ago I held you
newly born under a crescent moon,
and gave you the name which means *servant*
of God, and I did not speak of tanks,
the thunder of iron, missiles flying
over the rooftops of our city – I whispered
the call to prayer once in each ear.

It should not be like this. Abd Allah,
many years from now, your own children
should wash your body three times
after your death. They should seal your mouth
with cotton, reciting prayers in a wash
of light and grieving, a perfume of lemons
and jasmine on your skin.

It should not be like this, Abd Allah.
I wanted you to see the Ctesiphon Arch,
the Tower of Samarra, the Ziggurat of Ur.
I wanted to show you the Arabic language
written on the spines of the sawtooth mountains.
I wanted to teach you our family history,
and see where you might take it.

I cannot undo what the shrapnel has done.
I climb down into the crumbling earth
to turn your face toward Mecca, as it must be.
Remember the old words I have taught you,
Abd Allah. And go with your mother,
buried here beside you – she will know the way.

The Inventory from a Year Lived Sleeping with Bullets

Rifle oil, *check*. Smoke grenades, *check*. Desert boots, *check*. Plates of body armor, *check*. The list ongoing – combat patrols added, 5 Paragraph Op Orders, mission briefs, nights spent staring for heat signatures through the white-hot lens, lasers bore-sighted to the barrels they guide. The conceptual and physical given parallel structure.

A dead infant. A night-crushed car. A farmer slumped over a Toyota steering wheel near an Army checkpoint. A distraught relative staring beyond, pieces of brain on the dashboard. The refusal to render aid. The fresh dark soil over the bodies.

The boredom. The minutes. The hours. Days. Weeks. Months. The moments unbound by time's dominion. The years after.

Torture fragments. A man pissing on the Qu'ran. A man at a rifle range firing a bullet. A bullet carrying the middle vowel of the word *Inshallah*. A combat load of ammunition.

3rd Squad. 1st Platoon. Blackhorse Company. The faces – ones I hated and the ones I loved. Even the ones I don't remember. And all who don't remember me. *Contact. Three O'Clock. 50 meters. Talk the Guns.*

And Seattle at night. Rain drizzling down. First weekend home from war. Sgt. Gould sucking a woman's nipple in the cuddle room at the rave party. Glow sticks in mouths, a language of light. A language I don't recognise. A man in an Energizer bunny suit, on roller-skates, bass pounding the camouflage of tireless eternal Easter followed by a brunette in black leather bustier, thigh-high wet leather PVC boots, her eyes the dark carbon from the barrel's chamber as she pulls a leashed man by the throat. These people. *My people.*

Put it all in the rucksack. Throw the rucksack on your back and call it your *house*. Do a commo check with anyone out there in the bush, listening. Do a commo check back home. Get your shit on straight. *Stay Alert and Stay Alive*. Drink water and conduct your PCIs. We've reached the *Line of Departure*. So lock and load, man. From here on out we are on radio silence.

৶

I was called out into a field of compassion
into a universe of billions of souls

JOHN BALABAN

The Mutanabbi Street Bombing

March 5, 2007

In the moment after the explosion, an old man
staggers in the cloud of dust and debris, hands
pressed hard against bleeding ears
as if to block out the noise of the world
at 11.40 A.M., the broken sounds of the wounded
rising around him, roughened by pain.

Buildings catch fire. Cafés.
Stationery shops. The Renaissance Bookstore.
A huge column of smoke, a black anvil head
pluming upward, fueled by the *Kitah al-Aghani*,
al-Isfahani's *Book of Songs*, the elegies of Khansa,
the exile poetry of Youssef and al-Azzawi,
religious tracts, manifestos, translations
of Homer, Shakespeare, Whitman, and Neruda –
these book-leaves curl in the fire's
blue-tipped heat, and the long centuries
handed down from one person to another, verse
by verse, rise over Baghdad.

ع

As the weeks pass by, sunsets
deepen in color over the Pacific. Couples
lie in the spring fields of California,
drinking wine, making love in the lavender
dusk. There is a sweet, apple-roasted
smell of tobacco where they sleep.
They dream. Then wake to the dawn's
early field of lupine – to discover themselves
dusted in ash, the poems of Sulma
and Sayyab in their hair, Sa'di on their eyebrows,
Hafiz and Rumi on their lips.

In memory of Mohammed Hayawi

Eucalyptus

The grace of the world survives our intervention
HARRY MATTISON

As dawn approaches the city of Mosul, a dense fog
hangs in the eucalyptus grove.
                                 Water buffalo
lift their heads from the belly-high grass, nostrils
wet and shining, to breathe in the damp smell of earth,
the ammunition belts and army winter coats
left rotting in the park these many years.
                                      In the fog,
among the grass-covered berms of old tank emplacements,
tree trunks take on the shadowy forms
of men, women, children
                         who are coming closer,
perhaps, or moving away – it's difficult to tell,
these shadows in the half-light of dawn,

who have found the small bright lanterns of sunlight
breaking through the leaves above.

In the Tannour Oven

Stitched into the gutted belly of the calf:
a fat young lamb, dressed and cleaned,
its organs removed from the cave of bone.
And within the lamb: a stuffed goose.
And in the goose's belly: a mortar round.
And within the mortar round: a stuffed hen.
And in the hen's belly: a grenade.
And within the grenade: a stuffed thrush.
In the thrush: a .50 caliber bullet.
In the .50 caliber bullet: seasoned
with murri, oil, and thyme – a wedding ring.

Ah, love – when you undo the stitches,
take your time. I have love letters
stuffed inside of me, these tiny bodies
made heavy by their own labored breathing.

Study of Nudes by Candlelight

You are the water pouring into water,
steam rising in the heat of the bath
to coat me in a film of light,
as mirrors surround us with portraits
of the infinite, receding versions
of you turning toward me, as if
I can see from this day forward,
how you carry my shadow in the gloss
of your skin, without complaint, the promise
of light dripping from your fingers,
your wine-dark nipples, my lips
kissing your own, farther and farther away.

In the Guggenheim Museum

We follow Frank Lloyd Wright's rotunda
with our hands herringboned together,
the curving ramp of galleries like the cochlea
of the inner ear, and she kisses me
on the rounded bone behind the earlobe –
a structure whose name I don't know –
before working our way through the crowd
of art-filled heads, their faces radiating
the blonde ale they drank at lunch
as they slur Kandinsky on their tongues, words
in lavender brushstrokes, conversations
trailing behind them like multi-colored scarves
which brush over our forearms and shoulders,
disconnected from their source –
mysterious, beautiful, fleeting.

At the entrance to the Sound and Light exhibit,
we read the poster board thoughts of the artist,
or maybe it's a typed message from someone
who once talked with the artist, or maybe
they simply wrote what they thought the artist
might say, or think, telling us *Remove Your Shoes*
to feel the carpet's texture, the floor's vibrations
in decibels below the threshold of human hearing,
a *No Speaking Zone*, a place for wavelengths
of visible light, tonal harmonics reconciling
the Precambrian structures of the brain,
oscillating through the millennia to converse
with our bipedal awkward face-to-face
making of love, which is all she and I
can think of now, the unified theory
of color conjoined with sound,
and she squeezes my hand tight in her own
under the wire-hung letters of language,
which rotate above us in a perfectly
destroyed state, the letter *C*, the letter *S*,
each letter stretched, bent a little out of plane,
as if the invisible paper of language had been
peeled away so that now they drift

over us, freed from the word *chair* or *staircase*,
vibrations of sound gently lifting the alphabet
and lowering it the way a breeze might lift
the tips of her hair, my fingers guiding
the zipper in its channel, tooth by tooth,
the way it did last night, in the park, long after
closing time when the sprinklers switched on
and we didn't stop – the killdeer singing, a siren
somewhere off in the distance, the sun itself
held at bay by the horizon, just long enough
to divot the soft lawn with her kneecaps
pressing down, shifting to the rocking of hips,
my own back given the imprint of earth
authored by the grass in its green vernacular,
muscles lifting, my thumbs at the iliac crest,
the smooth curve of her breast, the streetlamps
tapered like candles to backlight her silhouette
as we kissed the small quick fires from each other's
mouths, cold water falling in a graceful arc
from the sprinkler heads positioned around us,
her hair matted and tangling with it –
this is what I'm thinking about in the museum,
the skeletons of art hung around us, petrified,
staring through the hard lenses of framing and oil,
staring at us from their fossilised stations
in the past, in wonder, marveling at
these two lovers, here, each of us
fully given to the inexorable process
of death, and yet, here we are
walking among them – *alive.*

The One Square Inch Project

Deep in the Olympic National Park, where black trumpet mushrooms
rise from the deadfall and leaf rot, I follow the footpath
leading to silence.
                    It is a type of medicine by landscape,
this forgetting of my life – yesterday's drive up from Fresno,
the auburn leaves of mountain ash, variations of maple,
aspens in gold and rust and creamy yellows – all given to memory,
hushed by the green work of water; moss, vines, forest canopy.

An owl shakes the morning frost from its feathers.
Roosevelt Elk work their way through the pines up the slope.
Water, dripping from the leaves. Water, in tiny rivulets.

There is a small red stone placed exactly on the spot
where silence grows. It is a gift. It was given by the Elder
of the Quileute Tribe, David Four Lines, and I will not disturb it.
And I put nothing in the *Jar of Quiet Thoughts* nearby.
Because there is not one thing I might say to the world
which the world does not already know.

I sit. And I listen.
                    When I return to California,
to my life with its many engines – I find myself changed,
the city somehow muted, frenetic and fully charged with living, yes,
but still, when gifted with this silence, motions have more
of a dance to them, like fish in schools of hunger, once
flashing in sunlight, now turning in shadow.

NOTES

Epigraph (13) *(I embrace the frightful and the beautiful)* is by Abd
al-Wahhab al-Bayati (1926-99) from section five of his poem 'Trans-
formations of Aisha: Aisha's Birth and Death in the Magical Rituals
Inscribed in Cuneiform on the Nineveh Tablets', translated by
Saadi Simawe, *Iraqi Poetry Today: Modern Poetry in Translation*,
no. 19 (King's College London, 2003), 51.

Howl Wind (17)
Classical Poems by Arab Women, edited by Abdullah al-Udhari (Lon-
don: Saqi Books, 1999), 26.

Viking 1 (24)
Epigraph is from NASA's Mars Exploration Program webpage.

Al-A'imma Bridge (32)
The epigraph is a quote from President Jalal Talabani, 31 August
2005, from a CNN reported story ('Iraq Mourns Stampede Victims').
It was reported that 965 died and that over 400 were injured. Not
one shot was fired – someone in the crowd of worshippers was said
to have claimed a suicide bomber was among them, and panic ensued.
    Freaky Freaky is a slang term used to denote bootlegged porn
videos, copied onto blank disks and sold, usually, for one US dollar.
I personally had Iraqi children try to hawk all of the items men-
tioned in this poem as my unit would prepare to enter US bases in
Iraq, to include having children offer foil-wrapped packages they
hawked as 'Heroin'.

Guarding the Bomber (37)
In the Qur'an, it is said that at the very pit of Hell (known as
Jahannam or as *al-Nar*), there are a certain number of angels (the
number of angels will be debated, it says) – these angels have the
duty of keeping those condemned to Jahannam from escaping its
flames and hooks.

Madinat Al-Salam (54)
Madinat Al-Salam is part of the ancient city, which later became
known as Baghdad.
    Epigraph is from Amina Elbendary's article 'They Came To
Baghdad' (*Al-Ahram Weekly Online*, Issue No. 634, 17-23 April
2003).

Tell Me, Beautiful One, from Where Did the Lord Bring You? (57)
The title and its Arabic transliteration are by Douad Al-Kuwaity
(1910-76) and Saleh Al-Kuwaity (1908-86), from the album *Masters
of Iraqi Music* (ARC Music Productions Int. Ltd, released in 2008).
For more information on the killings, which took place outside
Mandali, Iraq on 24 October 2004, see Edward Wong's report in
the *New York Times*, 'Ambush Kills 50 Iraq Soldiers Execution
Style' (25 October 2004).

Insignia (52)
Epigraph is from the CBS Evening News story by Katie Couric
(17 March 2009), 'Sexual Assault Permeates U.S. Armed Forces'.

The Discothèque (62)
Pogues is a term some Army soldiers use to denote soldiers who
are, as they used to say, 'in the rear with the gear'. While reading
Fear Up Harsh: An Army Interrogator's Dark Journey Through Iraq,
by Tony Logouranis, I realised that I was connected to what he
speaks about in his book – I was one of the infantry soldiers handing
over captured detainees (prisoners) to the military police unit (MPs)
in Mosul (who would in turn hand over the prisoners and my
paperwork depositions to men and women like Tony).

Jundee Ameriki (64)
The epigraph is from Ahmad Shauqi's (1869-1932) poem 'In Exile',
Desmond O'Grady, *Ten Modern Arab Poets* (Dublin: Dedalus Press,
1992), 18. *Jundee Ameriki* is a transliteration of the Arabic for Amer-
ican soldier.

Ajal (67)
The Oxford Dictionary of Islam (Oxford: Oxford University Press,
2003), 12.

The Inventory from a Year Lived Sleeping with Bullets (68)
PCI stands for Pre-Combat Inspection.

Epigraph (69) *(I was called out into a field of compassion/ into a uni-
verse of billions of souls)* is from John Balaban's poem, 'At 4:00 A.M.
Asleep'. John Balaban, *Words for My Daughter* (Port Townsend,
WA: Copper Canyon Press, 1991).

The Mutanabbi Street Bombing (70)
The reference in this poem to *The Book of Songs* relates specifically to Abu al-faraj al-Isfahani's (*d.* 967) famous anthology, *Kitah al-aghani* (The Book of Songs). The poet Tumadir bint Amr ibn Ashsharid, better known as *Khansa* (*d.* 646 C.E.), was often asked by the Prophet Mohammad to recite her poetry. Zuhayr ibn Abi Sulma (*d. c.* 607) wrote his *Mu'allaqah* (a collection of elaborate, polythematic celebrations of tribal values), the means by which tribal conflicts in pre-Islamic Arabia might be resolved. Badr Shakir al-Sayyab (1926-64) was a pioneer of the *free verse* movement Iraq – his best known poem is 'Rainsong' and he has been called the 'Prophet of the 14 July 1958 Revolution' for the impact his poetry had on the people during that time. Roger Allen, *An Introduction to Arabic Literature* (Cambridge University Press, 2000).

Eucalyptus (71)
The epigraph by Harry Mattison was something I heard him say during the literary symposium: *Cry Havoc! Poetry of War and Remembrance, 1968-2008* (a Lannan Literary Symposium & Festival, Georgetown University, 30-31 March 2009).

In the Tannour Oven (72)
This poem is based, in part, on a recipe from the amazing book, Nawal Nasrallah's *Delights from the Garden of Eden: A Cookbook and a History of the Iraqi Cuisine* (AuthorHouse, 2003), 298. This was a book kindly sent to me through Books for Soldiers website while I served in Iraq with the US Army.